DEEP NORTH

BERT ALMON

DEEP NORTH

THISTLEDOWN PRESS

Canadian Cataloguing in Publication Data

Almon, Bert, 1943 -
  Deep North

Poems.
ISBN 0-920066-88-7 (bound).
ISBN 0-920066-89-5 (pbk.)

I. Title.
PS8551.L59D4 1984   C811'.54   C84-091156-4
PR9199.3.A45D4 1984

Book design by A.M. Forrie
Cover illustration by Martin Kathrens

Typesetting by Résistance Graphics, Edmonton
Set in 11 point Century Oldstyle

Printed and bound in Canada by
Hignell Printing Limited, Winnipeg

Thistledown Press
668 East Place
Saskatoon, Saskatchewan
S7J 2Z5

To Olga

ACKNOWLEDGEMENTS:

This book was completed with the assistance of a grant from The Canada Council.

Many of these poems previously appeared or will appear in:

Again, The Beloit Poetry Journal, Canadian Forum, Canadian Literature, Cross-Canada Writers' Quarterly, CV II, Dalhousie Review, Edmonton Bullet, The Literary Review, The Malahat Review, Manitoba Writers' Newsletter, Negative Capability, NeWest Review, New Quarterly, Northern Light, Prism International, Puerto del Sol, Quarry, San Marcos Review, This Magazine, Toronto Life, Whetstone.

Some of the poems were broadcast on Alberta Anthology.

"The Way to the Hot Springs" appears in the *Anthology of Magazine Verse and Yearbook of American Poetry* (Monitor Book Company).
"Signs Taken for Wonders"first appeared in *Aurora: New Canadian Writing 1980* (Doubleday).

This book was published with the assistance of The Canada Council, the Saskatchewan Arts Board, and Alberta Culture.

CONTENTS

I. MODERN TIMES

I. MODERN TIMES

CLIFFHANGER AT THE ROYAL ALEXANDRA

The big TV set in the waiting room
is tuned to a soap opera
and everyone is watching.
The men who coaxed a manic friend
into signing the admissions form
watch the blackmailer threaten
the parents of an adopted child.
A woman across from me rocks a small boy
on her lap. He holds a flowered towel
over one eye. She is watching,
he is watching with the other eye.
At the information desk a woman
on a stretcher calls number after number,
asking for a ride home. Between calls
she watches the pleading mother,
the angry father. Two policemen
come in with a man in a wheelchair.
The woman on the stretcher
picks up the phone once more.
I hear a gunshot on the set
and turn with the policemen
to watch the imaginary sufferings
of attractive people on the screen.

STARSHIP INVADERS

What do the hot-knifers and coke-sniffers know?
His habit is dropping quarters in the slot
and taking the levers, watching the starships
blink onto the screen, nine in rows of three,
then peel off row by row toward his planet.
He sends bright dots — laser torpedoes — against them,
erases each ship in a shower of flashes
to win the first match. The second speeds up,
the third he usually loses, the one that wins
a free game. Lunch money, paper route
and allowance go down the slot, so after hours
he has a job sweeping up the arcade
to earn a little more. In the back room
there's still a gaudy pinball machine
used by older people, but he despises
the materiality of it: the steel ball
rolling through baffles, the flippers
and buzzers. Starship Invaders is clean,
silent, a dance along printed circuits.
He has no time for lunches, for girls
and cars. This is pure, mind against the mind
of the machine. In his daydreams, the hands
moving at the controls are flashing lights.

FOR A FAILED BRUNETTE

Sharon,
a red-haired majorette,
dexterous twirler of batons.
In junior high school I talked to you once,
and the next day your boy friend Guy
threw me against a brick wall
in a two-handed gesture of rebuke.
In high school I talked to you again,
and your admirer Harry Welch
threw me against a concrete wall
and told me I'd better lay off, quick.

Red hair, but you never lost
your temper in your own person.
At the class reunion you told me
you'd become a psychoanalyst.
That day your hair was a muddy auburn:
for once you wanted to be a brunette.

I remember the college physics lab
and the tour of the anechoic chamber,
the walls that soaked up sound.
A joker in the class turned off the light
and you began screaming in an odd voice
purged of its overtones.
After I found the swinging light bulb
you told us that somebody
had started hitting you with a stick.
I'm ready to confess it wasn't me.
Perhaps psychology has explained it to you:
I know your daughter has never had twirling lessons.

After the reunion no one threw me against a wall,
not even my wife, and I was a little disappointed.
I can't remember if I ever yearned for you:
time sponges up what might have been important
along with almost everything that was.

THE JOURNEYMAN'S PRAYER

The faucet fitting disappears
into a hole above the sink.
It must be unscrewed from a pipe
inaccessible behind the wall.
He tries a channel lock,
the fitting begins to break
into pieces, he inserts
a huge screwdriver blade
to give the fitting substance,
then he utters the journeyman's prayer
as his veins and sinews bulge:
   GDMFCKNSMBTCH!
Straining has squeezed the words
down to consonants, gutturals
that conjure corroded threads
to give and command the steel
to stop flaking into splinters.
Again the prayer, again and again,
and as the threads unlock at last
he offers up the journeyman's psalm:
    AH!
a pure vowel in the hollow of the mouth.

TENNESSEE WALTZ

The song the words describe is the song itself
Patti Paige sang it on television tonight
in a Y dress: V-neck and vertical lines
to make her look slender in middle age

I find myself remembering part of a room
where a radio is playing somewhere
A boy works on an enormous puzzle —
a granite dome and its reflecting pool

He is assembling it on a woolen rug
The dome is finished and only its image
remains, the pieces that were so hard
to distinguish from the originals

The reflection is the same and different
I can see a pattern of woven flowers
where the carpet shows through the gap
The boy tries out pieces along the edge

I want to tell him to study carefully
the relation of the fact to its image
Someday the memories of what he has lost
will be everything he can keep

The radio playing out of my view
must be hot from its glowing tubes
I would like one more look at the carpet
before this picture trembles on the water

MORNING SOUNDS

A boy knows he has a father when he hears
the alarm go off across the hallway
at 4:30, before it's light outside,
and hears the pocket change and the key ring
scooped up from the wooden monkey pod
on his parents' dresser. Other sounds —
hands sudsing under the faucet with strong soap,
the sizzle of bacon that precedes the smell,
the snap of wax paper torn from the roll,
a bicycle scuffing up the gravel drive
that leads to the road to the refinery.

One morning my father came back right away
with a pain in his chest. The doctor arrived,
then my mother tiptoed into my room
to tell me it was double pneumonia.
I hardly knew what pneumonia was, but
I could hear the effort of his breathing
from across the hall, pushing a weight
on his chest: the infection, the bills
unpaid and the bills to come. One morning —
before my own alarm rang, the signal
for me to get up, dress and go to school.

THE REFINERY STRIKE OF '51

for Katie, who wanted to be a prole

Flimsy as it is, wood and paper,
a picket sign is an aching burden
in the hands of a striker with family.
Goons drove a car through the line once.
When my father got part-time work at a garage,
I came home from the aunt who was feeding me.
Who made the gasoline he was pumping?
The casuistry of need is simple:
ask no questions and keep paying the rent.
I would go see him at lunch and have the treat
of a soft drink: a gaudy color never seen
in nature pulled by its cap from the machine.
There: I've made it a happy poverty,
but now I count every nickel resting
on my father's greasy palm. Strawberry
was the favorite, a pure red, the bottle
sweating with cold in the heat of the sun.

THE SMELL OF ETHER

My mother always hated that smell
A whiff of it while visiting hospitals

I thought it was her Caesareans
she was remembering with nausea

until she told me about her aunt
who'd had so many abortions

Once things were so advanced
the ether was necessary

In a spare room of the house
the same evening a suitor was coming

A suitor coming for my mother
Would he notice and what would he notice

The aunt died many years later
after refusing surgery to save her life

unwilling to be touched again
A wild growth reached its term

(The suitor never noticed
but my mother always noticed

in hospital corridors a whiff of ether
long after it dropped out of use)

THE INTRUSIONS

Since the age of five, when the ambulance
took her mother away for a last operation,
she never liked anyone coming to the door
and would even cry when the ice cream man,
dressed in white like an attendant,
pedalled down the street on his cart.
As a housewife, she feared the scissors man,
stooped as he was, almost deaf, snotty nose
and handkerchief the year around.
The thought of letting him in the house
and trusting him with sharp edges —
scissors, knives, any blade at all —
left her weak all over. She met him
at the door each time with a quarter
for a packet of needles, to put away
on the sewing machine cabinet, unopened
and folded in three around itself
with its hundreds of tiny points.

SNOW WHITE RETURNS TO THE FOREST

1

Coming to the city to meet me
you saw a black bear beside the road
and took it for a favorable omen.

Driving to the city to meet you, I passed
through a dry thunderstorm, and saw a grass fire
burning by the road, the visible mark of lightning.

2

Why should we want to meet again?
We were deafened and blinded by our storm,
but now we've regained our senses, no point
in warming our hands by a little fire.

3

Lady of the Woods, I've touched you again:
can I go back to heavy sleep in a narrow cave?
I'm sweating in my thick fur, and my bones ache
in a clear flame, the invisible mark of lightning.

INTERMEZZO

1

"Wait right here, don't move," you said.
You had sixty seconds to reach the switch
that turned off the alarm system.
But the burglar was already on the premises,
his appraiser's eye looking over nothing you've insured.
With snowy shoes he stood on the mat,
counting back from sixty, a hundred, from what number.

2

Over cups and cups of coffee
we talked about everyone we know:
him, and her, what this one
thinks about that one's husband.
Gossip always sweetens the cup.
When the pot was empty
we had covered everybody —
no, I can think of two
we didn't mention at all.

3

"It's going to be an early spring this year,"
your friend said, after one look at your face.
A few streets away the pipe-laying crews
are burning huge heaps of straw
to loosen the frozen ground,
conspirators in a prophecy.

1

Where I'm from
lint picked off someone's garment
can be surrendered for a kiss.
You've worn your blue dress
today, you're full of static,
and I came, my pockets full of lint,
ready to plant it on you,
when all I have to do
is pick you threadbare, threadbare.

2

What words did you hear
out of my confusion?
Ruthless, relentless.
I meant ruthless
like March sun on a snowbank,
relentless
like the part you've taken
in an old play: Strength.
Is there a role for me,
Folly, perhaps, or Carelessness,
or Apology in his shabby costume?

3

And here is one of my braver speeches:

I'm a few grains of sleep in your eyes
the residue of a night of strange dreams
There, you've wiped them away

4

I carry a poem in my coat pocket
written by a friend who isn't a poet
which is why I keep touching it
like a ticket to a concert in heaven
or a safe conduct from the higher authorities
(the ones I've never believed in
though now I'm sure they've stamped my pass)
The seal is too faint to read
but I can feel it on her notepaper
whenever I reach into my pocket

5

The inflections of Greek verbs and nouns
are posted on notecards over the sink
so that you can drill yourself on ancient grammar
while handling wet dishes. The blue ink
has blurred in places where the water splashed.
I'm only a scholar of the modern tongues,
what have I been learning by heart? Lessons
of your bed upstairs: the conjugation of sighs,
the sweet declensions of the pronouns *you* and *I.*

6

I want to find the spots
where you dab your perfume
I seek them out like a bee
drifting over morning roses
Here, and here, yes
but if there are others
I'll never find them
with the whole world
turning to fragrance
as I skim your white horizons

MOTOR SKILLS

The IQ test called me a verbal genius,
a manual idiot, which averaged out
to bright/normal. The blind men in the fable
at least knew there was an elephant,
but I was left with all the puzzle parts
jumbled on the table when the time was up
and hadn't distinguished his tail from his trunk.

But if you give me a practical test,
ask me to shape a remembered body
in the air, then I'll shut my eyes and hold
the width of your face between my hands
and move it gently toward my own,
or I'll wrap my arms precisely around
the circuit of your companionable waist.

This boast from your bright/normal lover.

PHONE BOOTH POEMS

1

Calling you from a quiet street
I discover after you answer
that rush hour has just ended
and every peak-time bus
will rumble by me on the way
to the garage for the night
Each bus reminds me of a person
with some opinion of our love
like SOUTHGATE going by just now
with gnashing gears and puffing brakes
Yes I'll have to talk a little louder

2

Once as I was dialing your number
I looked out at the full moon rising
and saw how close and orange it was
I almost thought I could touch it
Later as I was driving back home
it was pale and shrunken in the sky
and about equally distant
from both of our houses

3

I remember having to buy coffee
because I needed a quarter to call you
Part of my change was a crisp dollar bill
The pretty girl who counted it out
asked if I had a pencil with me
"I know a good trick
for breaking a pencil
with a new dollar bill"

If I speak cautiously
it's because I might have a knack
for snapping a heart with a quarter
your heart or my heart

I sleep in a room where a telescope
stands with its eye buried in the curtains.
There are yellow roses by the bed, a gift
from one woman. I have a card with reproofs
and arguments from another. In the living room
I graze on a stack of the New York Times,
reading about the world as it was last month
while catching up on myself. My host
stays up at night talking to me
about the need to save the soul,
but he knows better than to tell me how.
(A soul weighs about seven grams,
according to the Harvard Medical School,
where bodies were weighed before and after
the last breath: a fact from the Science Column.)

In the room next to mine a guinea pig
burrows in a box of wood shavings
and its own droppings. I prefer the budgie
in the atrium: it sings when it hears
children's voices and running water,
murmurs of the jungle. The guinea pig is dying:
its tiny feet bleed from clawing at the box.
The bird flies out of its open cage
from time to time, a feathered kamikaze
that always misses as it ranges the house.
I have to choose one life or another, but now
I just make a little rain forest music
in the sink as I wash up after supper.

COUNTING YOUR SMILES

If I tried to catalogue your smiles
I'd start with the one when you see me
the one with the whole body behind it

There's the slightly tilted smile
when you're going to ask a question
I'm going to find it hard to answer

And the smile of goodbye
when I want you to be cheerful
It clenches pain in lines around your eyes

Or the way you shut those eyes
to think about something important
Not a gesture of the lips but counting as a smile —

you see why I could never finish the list.

Here it is a frosty November
and the man who paints on velvet
still sits in a lawn chair
on the lot of the boarded-up Texaco
hawking the rows of pictures:
mountains sunsets and roses
John Lennon with and without Beatles
and those adorable Eskimo children

Every time I walk by I shiver
at the nude on the sunny beach
She doesn't seem to feel the wind
but I wonder what the man would say
if I asked him to paint her a sweater

A FORMAL SITTING

The photographer's assistant
is really the boss   Fat
with thinning hair   friendly
with everyone but the photographer
a tall woman from Taiwan

I resent his arranging
of my body and limbs
He puts one of my feet up
on a square of foam rubber
places my hands on thighs
says   Don't move now

It's the undertaker's manner
I dislike   laying out the body
for an eternity on film
Now I must relax and smile
without moving a millimetre

The photographer isn't pleased
She comes over and brushes back
a single strand of hair
My rigor eases to this touch
but I know that the flash
will catch me with eyes shut

FAIR WARNING

The woman at Sears sold my wife
a plastic tray of zinnias. One
looked a little odd, but the clerk
said it was a blue zinnia, rare
and splendid, wait and see.
In a month it was pushing
the other flowers out of bed
and showed clusters of seeds
but no blossoms of any color.
I decided to pull it up,
and was left with four blisters
on my hand. Woman of Sears,
when I open my pet shop
I'm going to sell your kids
a garter snake with rattles.

SECURITY GUARD. ADULT MOTEL

I just sit by the night clerk's desk
letting the pistol show and work
on my thesis: pupil-teacher ratios
in junior high school. No one makes
trouble, the customers are solid types,
at our prices. We offer them mirrors,
water beds, colour TV with blue channels,
shower stalls big enough for four.
I keep the gun loaded but the chamber
empty. If I got careless settling
a ruckus, the Department of Education
would never give me a credential.
The desk clerk hates the gay couples,
but I feel a little queasy about men
who check in alone. I imagine them
huffing and puffing to inflate rubber dolls.
The manager got mad when I kidded him
and said we could rent dolls ourselves:
"What do you think this is, a whorehouse?"
Next year it's social studies all day
at a school full of rowdy kids who neck
in the halls or smoke dope in the john.
Some days I'll miss wearing the 45.

The French talk about seven colors
seven musical notes seven flavors
and the Seven Great Sauces
(not to mention the Forty Immortals)

So naturally every twenty years or so
they reorganize the universe
along existential lines
or into the raw and the cooked
or as signifieds that become new signifiers

My American father-in-law
heats all the leftovers in one pot
which saves a lot of washing up
and tells me about his own father
who'd mix everything on the plate
and then add a slice of pie
"Sometimes for good measure
he'd pour in his coffee and say
it all gets mixed together anyway"

When I'm told to recook everything
by the latest Parisian recipe
I remember the great French gourmet
whose favorite restaurant cut a crescent
out of a table to accommodate his girth
and I prefer that dash of coffee
— a gesture of barbaric panache

Tenpo Reformation came about as a result of the
law to prevent the making of beautiful kites.
From this time to the present calligraphy was
used to decorate the kites. The calligraphy
of the dragon who is God of water is quite chic
even in modern times.

Plastic Art in the Sky

Think of the new frontiers
for bureaucracy:
the Manifesto on Birthday Parties
with a Codicil on Candles
and the Statutes for Gardeners
with special penalties for roses

Or better yet, think
of the bureaucrat, a tacky dragon
who is God of ink
raging in memos over the failure
of the Decree on the Uniformity of Snowflakes

EPICUREAN

She opens new books
right in the middle
and takes a deep sniff

— Doesn't everyone do it
she says to my question
— That smell of fresh paper

Some sybarites would pine away
on bread and water
Others would send out invitations

TEACHER'S DREAM

As an adviser I keep the cliches
on the steam table till they turn to mush,
and then I serve them up. In my dream
a student tells me she wants to enroll
in graduate school but can't afford the fees.
Why don't you live in the past, I tell her,
everything was so much cheaper then.
Do you mean go to school in the past,
or live there and commute, she responds.
Well, you could also consider marriage,
two can study as dearly as one. At that,
she turns and speeds off on roller skates.
I wake with small wheels spinning behind my eyes.

BROADER HORIZONS

for Rhona McAdam

My librarian friend tells me
there are places in the cataloging rules
to classify extra-terrestrial life
"Nothing alien is alien to me"
will be the new transhumanist motto

We'll learn about chlorine biochemistry
and sense organs that can detect
the genuine music of the spheres
(cross-reference with sculpture
and gravitational mechanics)

But then I think of my neighbors coming
with one of their grumbling petitions
worried about real estate values
"Do you really want someone next door
whose breath smells like a swimming pool?"

A cord stretched near the ceiling
held the grade six art projects,
the human dream of flight dangling
in red construction paper models:
planes and rockets, even a balloon
with its basket hung from paper ropes.
My daughter's project was four rooms
of a house, strung trainwise on the cord.
I stood on tiptoes to look in
and she proudly told me how she'd made
the furniture. "But I didn't leave
enough room to walk around the sink."
"But what is it, Cathy, how does it fit
the assignment?" "It's a flying house,
someday everybody will have one."
When I turned to her desk, I saw
a neat pile of grey eraser crumbs,
gatherings of a month. "They're soft,
feel them." She had hoarded her mistakes
and changes in tactile form. I doubted
that I would learn much from her workbooks.
Her thoughts are never on lined paper.

THE BREAK-UP

Walk in thawing wind to the river bank
a trail of mud and trampled weeds
a hand to help her down to the brink

Ice slips away like broken meringue
the current is faster than you thought
eating at the broken floes that remain

Nothing much to show a lady
a bored and winded woman
so she climbs back unaided

You stay to count the floes
making guesses at the erosion
then you follow her, and know

the river will be clear tomorrow

No, the dog wasn't bleeding

When the Doberman looked out
and saw a skunk feeding from his dish
he went right through the screen

Then he spent the morning
rubbing his nose in the dirt
till his master brought tomato juice

The red bath was another humiliation
so he cleared the wrought iron fence
and spread a scent of wildness

through the crescents of Griffin Heights

PALACE OF ILLUSION

for Minnette

You enjoyed the fluttering birth
of doves from rippled handkerchiefs

and the lady cut in half by a saw
so sharp it never touched her,

but the big act, behind velvet
curtains, under purple light:

the tattooed man, a neural freak
who drove a nail up one nostril,

smiled, then inserted a screwdriver
into the other, dark ichor running

in the heavy light, and as finale
(your eyes were shut now, unbearable

for you the pain he couldn't feel)
offered to pass a safety pin through

bunched flesh of his arm, and snap it shut.
Perhaps you should have watched, to learn

the lesson of the festering sores on his skin:
suffering unfelt is suffering that mutilates.

THE SMALLEST DETAILS

You could call him cautious, or timid:
prudent is the word that he'd select.
He wears a red shirt to eat spaghetti
and for the colder nights he turns on
the electric blanket a little early
and puts his pajamas under it to warm.
But when he goes to meet her — the joker,
the casual one who sets his ways down
to a sign of the zodiac — he forgets
his gloves, scarf, hat, and once even
fumbled his keys into a snowbank.

"Will you walk out of the air, my lord?"

The fine tuning won't prevent
channel 4 from drifting into 3
as a faint background
so that *Hamlet* is haunted
by ghostly figures
of the Coyote and the Roadrunner

As Hamlet says *"To be or not to be"*
I can make out the Coyote climbing
a ladder suspended in mid-air
Convention says he won't fall
until he tops the ladder and looks down
He'll smash on the desert floor
and come back renewed in another frame

Hamlet finishes his soliloquy
and greets the fair Ophelia
The Coyote has built a bomb
and lights the fuse
He has no trouble taking arms
while Hamlet is the man who looks down
and knows that resurrection
is not a convention of his play
We share his terror
rung by rung

II. DEEP NORTH

A LECTURE IN ECONOMICS

The airport lunch counter
has a sticky top
The busboy stands with a cloth
listening to the cashier
explain the price of gold
when to buy and when to sell

A man in a mauve turban
is eyeing the hot dog grill
uncertain of the meat
I bought a 90 cent Danish
thinking it was a 70 cent tart
so I'm twenty cents down
The cashier says sell the gold
before a price rise peaks

Walking out I find a dime —
that leaves me ten cents down —
but considering what I've learned
the tuition was quite reasonable

A man on the pier in Halifax
asks the black child eating ice cream,
"Is it good, son?" "Sure is, captain."
I think I'm on the wharf in Texas again,
with my grandfather, the maritime guard,
and Bootsie, his vicious bitch.
The black stevedores always called him
Captain Jack. Bootsie always growled.

There's a police strike on
and in the china shop
the owner is explaining
the alarm system to a customer:
"We have so many blacks here
I can't take any chances."
I imagine a thief coming
with swathes of tissue paper
and running away very gently
with a Delft figurine.

On Gottingen Street private guards
are patrolling with dogs
and the shop windows are boarded up.
After three days posters and graffiti
have improved the plywood,
giving the street a bright facade.
The city learns to cope with its problems,
the best way not to solve them.

FALL OF LOUISBOURG/FALL OF THE CARLETON HOTEL

Like a peasant living in the smithereens
of empire and robbing stones from the temple
to wall his orchard, Chief Clerk Bulkeley
had blocks of stone from Fortresse Louisbourg
shipped over to Halifax to build his house,
now the Carleton Hotel, where I stayed two weeks.
I've seen the careful replica on the coast —
the King's Bastion, the Porte Dauphine
but I've been deeper in history than that
by spending a fortnight in the Carleton.
Every morning I awoke to find more paint shards
fallen from the wall into the lidless toilet,
so that I thought if I stayed long enough
the original stones of the fortress would show.
I had no touches of imperial grandeur
in my slumber in spite of the drumbeats
of the rock band next door: I only dreamed
banal scenes of my distant home and family,
like a peasant soldier in an outpost of empire.

TRAIN. SYDNEY/HALIFAX

Two Cape Breton farm girls
who have to be called strapping
are off for a weekend in Halifax
With cut-off jeans and backpacks
they sit in the bar section
telling dirty jokes
to the elderly conductor
The blonde has a laugh
that sounds like hiccuping

When I took this train
from Halifax to Sydney
a disturbed woman
stood crying at the exit
and wouldn't get off
Her family cajoled and pleaded
then managed with shoving

I always see such lost people
but I see the others too
and the proper subversion of authority
The brunette who has to be called buxom
walking down the aisle to the john
wearing the conductor's hat

TWILIGHT. PICTOU HARBOR

The harbor is a drowned river valley
I find the best view in town by sitting
at the end of a grain terminal pier

A smoking pulp mill on the other shore
becomes picturesque in the twilight
At the harbor mouth the lighthouse
— count seven between its flashes —
is framed by two sailboats
one with green stripes on its canvas

At my left workmen hammer and drill
on a freighter that seems made of rust

Everything I contemplate is working
The cormorant skimming the water
— pothook neck and inky wings —
hunts for supper and will swallow it whole

Who at the pulp mill would believe it
but I am working too as I sit here

Down at Stellarton the miners
once dug coal from broken seams
— stellar coal that burns in starry sparks
With only the lightest sweat on my face
I search for the hidden sparks in things
and I know what it's like to have a seam break off
to realize that it continues in another layer

The wind pipes up and the sailboats head in
I see the freighter is strung with lights
that went on while I was looking away

1   the succession of marsh grasses

Cord grass, on salt mud flats.

Samphire and the amaranths,
in the true marsh condition.

With drainage and cleansing from salt,
timothy, couch grass, and red-top.
Also red and white clovers, oxeye daisies.

Someday wheat grows,
a transfigured grass.

2   the culture of wheat

You can see the Acadian fields from Grand Pré.
Their creation was almost a natural process:
dykes of piled logs, the wooden clapper valves
keeping the sea out while letting sweet water
of the rains rinse the salt from the marshes.
Volunteer grasses colonized the draining soil
and one day it was ready to be turned,
ready for the sowing of wheat, a grain
not well suited to the Nova Scotia climate.

Peasants could cross the ocean on trust
and not be able to imagine life without bread,
part of the Sacrament, part of the curse,
and something to pray for daily,
along with deliverance from evil.

3   the succession of fields

These lands came into the hands of strangers.
I know that flesh is grass,
but the displacement of grasses
in a dyked meadow is silent.
There are no commands, no lamentations,
and above all no howling of dogs.

Colonel Winslow, with his fine Puritan soul,
loaded the people on ships while deploring
"This painful task of so many heart-breaking scenes."

Like a rehearsal for our century:
those who died of privations on shipboard,
those who were parted from children in Massachusetts,
those who were sold into servitude in the Carolinas
or into outright slavery in Georgia.
Governor Lawrence assured the Lords of Trade
that "the vessels were hired at the cheapest rates."
Place 300 people in a room 24 feet by 18
and a death rate of 50% or more will arise
without particular acts of violence.

As the saline level drops,
samphire gives way to timothy.

But for weeks the cattle came in the evenings
to the ashes of Grand Pré
and the watch dogs howled all night.

To me "fort" means a palisade
of pointed stakes, Indians circling,
not the earthworks of Vauban,
his system of the dry ditch, bastions
and ravelins. I'm uneasy walking
these grassy slopes, gentle
as they are, quiet as it is,
a park now. I think the reason
must be the resemblance
to a graveyard, the green mounds,
the way that even in death
we remake the world in shapes
of living bodies. A gardener
mows the dry ditch by letting
the mower slide down hill,
then hauling it up with a cable.
He has been doing this all day,
though neither the French
nor the Indians are expected.

Along St. Mary's Bay
I saw the flag everywhere
Vertical bars of blue, white and red
with a small gold star in the blue
Along Baie Ste-Marie
the people everywhere
Doucets, Comeaus and LeBlancs
names from the mailboxes by the road
The families that slipped back in
after the Expulsion

In St. Bernard a stone church
as big as a cathedral serves a village
At Church Point the highest steeple
in North America looks down on a village
Buildings that proclaim the Acadian motto
On est venus c'est pour rester
to travelers on Highway 7

At Saulnierville Mme Thibodeault
sold me a dozen chocolate cookies
and was vague about the flag
"Last year people came by and said
it was the sign of this place"

The flag is the French tricolor
with a star for the Assumption
of the Blessed Virgin Mary
a peculiar conjunction of symbols
Heaven brought down to Earth
Earth ascending to Heaven
which must leave them right here
where the real flag of a people
is the lines of wash near the highway
snapping in the face of a traveler
saying we've come here to stay

Under candy-striped tents in the park
national tables offer food and crafts
from the old countries
                              Swedish pancakes
in cream, a Ukrainian woman using
wax and dye to create embroidered eggs
their intricate texture a reminder
we're all a happy mosaic here

But at the Chilean stand
there's a certain awkwardness
when people look at the wall hangings
the little cloth cut-outs
arranged in scenes from the homeland:
the secret police frisking a suspect
children eyeing a huge bottle of milk
impounded by a barbed wire fence
Some bits of the mosaic want to tell us
how they were formed in such jagged shapes
and in what ovens their enamel grew hard

III. WESTERN ROADS

LA PLUME DE MA TANTE

I was making plans
for my newspaper,
a flimsy tabloid
serving the Prairies.
I knew I was dreaming
after I chose the name —
Le Coureur de Bois —
and ordered a press run
of a million copies.

When the bell went off,
Pavlov's cat jumped
on my chest, buzzing
for its breakfast,
while I tried to count
how many years
I'd lived in Edmonton
without noticing French
spoken on the street.

Saskatchewan 14

What makes this grey and yellow autumn
unendurable isn't the dried thistles
in the right of way nor the rusted cars
by old farmhouses shedding their shingles
It's the one thin donkey intently grazing
in what looks like a field of bare earth

Local Attractions

Wainwright had the world's biggest buffalo
but I couldn't see it from the bus
so I can't say if it was alive or dead

Cut Knife had the world's biggest tomahawk
The Indians in front of the pool hall surely knew
where it's kept but the bus drove right past them

The world's biggest decorated easter egg
can be seen from the road at Vegreville
Keep your eyes on the stripe and you'll miss it

No Stopping on Shoulder

Passing through Hillsboro
we saw a fence full of morning glories
their faces open to the east
We gave them just the right interval —
some splendors should be glimpsed —
by dropping down to second gear
then easing back to third and fourth
We knew that the sun they faced
would be waiting for us in the west

A FEW FEATHERS

I like to watch barnyard birds
The long strides of the pecking hens
The doltish wanderings of turkeys
The way the geese walk with a floating gait
sure of their dignity but hopelessly droll

The geese are my favorites
Like a wandering coffee klatch
they inspect and chatter over everything
The matriarch hisses at strangers
with a great show of aggression
Vasilis comes along with his homemade bow
and tells me he shot a turkey in the neck
The turkey doesn't look the worse for it

When a coyote came into the yard one night
Vasilis's Uncle Ivan shot it with a rifle
"Did I skin it afterward? The bullet I used
was so big I skinned it with that"
I see the entire poultry yard sheltered
under the wings of his easy-going laugh

COUNTRY WESTERN BAR

A horseshoe nailed over the stage
The stage framed by buffalo skulls
Music pounding from the amplifiers

The singer is a small town auctioneer
Between songs he talks very fast
and he never stumbles over lyrics

The dancers on the wooden floor
turn everything to two-steps and polkas
It is all clean fun
I see two girls at the band table
start to get up and dance together
but giggling they sit down again
No one would think much about it
There is one good-looking fellow
who dances with the fat women in the place
He has a Swiss army knife on his belt
and is looking for a seventeenth attachment
His partners all have a sweaty good time

The woman across the table from me
has just ordered a glass of milk
The list has Bedhoppers and Electric Bananas
but just about everybody is drinking beer
at Duster's on a Saturday night
where a horseshoe hangs over us
Pull out the nails and I think
the lead guitar could keep it floating
or even start it bobbing in a little two-step

BRUTUS AND BIGFOOT.   BATTLE RIVER VALLEY

I can see Brutus through the farmhouse window
a lighted dragline gouging coal
from the strip mine across the highway
Brutus runs twenty-four hours a day
Bigfoot his brother has every other Sunday off
They stand in the grey hills they have made
— the landscape chewed down to grit
At night they are revolving Christmas trees
with eminent domain over the valley

A farmer is showing me his collection
of arrowheads and stone hammers that came up
year by year in the fields and meadows
He keeps them in a willow basket
bought from a half-breed woman
He has a flinty spirit himself
but relaxes turning the stones in his hands

The wife has shown me her surviving china
in the glass-fronted cabinet
that rests next to the woven basket
The fanciest pieces were a Christmas present
just after they married fifty years ago
The log cabin was so cold a cup in winter
would sometimes break under the shock of coffee
but they had no other dishes
I wonder how she has preserved her delicate manners

Whenever the man and woman look out the window
they can see the two brothers working
By 1999 this farm will go into the hopper
Every artifact of clay and stone will vanish
as the earth is peeled back to the Cretaceous
The Indians and Metis would tell us
that Bigfoot and Brutus are children of ours
How can we cut them out of the will
when they work so hard for their inheritance

1   Sprocket
the sound
it makes

sprocket

2   Even the teeth
of the smallest dog
can reach your ankle

3   Look at those fools playing tennis in the rain
I say to myself as I pedal by them

4   Grass clippings in streaks
across the small park
I see a squirrel standing
on two legs
Mowing day in Lilliput

5   At the Catholic school
for wayward girls
a nun in black
walks a well-trimmed
and leashed white poodle

6   Three good views of the valley
along the trail
no bench at the best one

7   The high school wall
spray painted
   Menage Et Trois
   All the Way
At least they're learning French
now if they'd learn it right

8   A copious cuff
chokes the chain

9   I watch the sunset in the east
on window after window after window

10   At dusk
the stadium across the river
is a pair of concrete jaws
edged with mercury vapor teeth
Suddenly it sends a roar
straight up to the moon

BLOCK PARTY

Once a year, with permits from the police
and the Liquor Control Board, we celebrate
mid-summer and get to know one another
as the kids play in the barricaded street.
Last year someone brought photographs
of the neighborhood when it was still wheat.
I saw the stream that explains the dip
in my sidewalk. I'm right on the vanished bank
as I talk to Mrs. Price and Mrs. LeBlanc,
two widows. Mrs. Price shivers in the night air
and sticks her hands under Mrs. LeBlanc's blouse
to warm. "Estelle, I can feel *rolls*."
"Marge, with a little more fat on your bones
you wouldn't be so cold." And then Estelle
goes on with the story of her daughter
and the rapist, how he threw her down in the snow.
"She thought it was a friend cutting up, that's why
she didn't yell at first, then she couldn't yell
because she was out of breath. Do you know
who saved her? I swear to God it was Denis,
looking down from heaven." "You mean the saint?"
I ask. "No, her brother, the one who died,
she prayed to him, and she got away. That boy
attacked five women in one month, and beat them up.
He was fifteen. But it was Denis who saved Monique:
absolutely nothing happened, the doctors told me."
I find I'm shivering myself, ankle-deep in the stream,
having daughters myself. I want to know how
that could be absolutely nothing, but it's time to go,
all along the street the doors are shutting.
I see the scorned wisdom of the middle class:
trust a good lock on a strong door
more than all the saints in heaven.
A three year old skates by, singing "Clementine,
lost and gone forever, darling Clementine."

The Chinook wind has stripped
the snow from some of the fields,
others show short stubble yellow
through the white. Wooden posts
and fence wire have a chaste style
at right angles. Where a hill
has blocked the wind, a truck sits
up to its flat hood in snow.
It may cough awake in spring.
Such views fight the spell
of freeway hypnosis, and
the faulty speedo cable helps:
unoiled, it chirps like a bird.
After fifty miles you crave
to see something living,
but settle for a road sign,
the yellow diamond
with a black deer, running.

THE WAY TO THE HOT SPRINGS

The buses show destination signs
that flash by like a friendly greeting,
and I want to honk my horn, blink
my lights, but that could be mistaken
for a warning instead of the spirit
of spring. I'm on my way to soak out
the aches of a winter's shoveling snow
in water heated by the planet's core.
If a little April snow from the hill
has slid down by the pool, I'll be tempted
to roll around in it, then take the plunge.
I was warned once that the shock could bring on
cardiac arrest, but everything I see
along the road stops me between beats,
like that cow wading right into the slough
to drink, followed gingerly by her calf.

As I drive south through Fort MacLeod
my landmark isn't the RCMP Museum
but the building I noticed the first time
as an immigrant just landed at Coutts
THE AMERICAN HOTEL — FULLY MODERN
An oddity I thought then, wondering most
about the fully modern   Dumb questions
from tourists gotten or expected?

Now I think it was just the style
of an earlier time, the sign lettered
in script of the 30's or 40's
On main street Claresholm today I saw
one store still boasting AIR CONDITIONING

Back then I didn't know the history
of the fort and the mounted police
or about the invasion from the south
I was recapitulating that day
though with no trader's whiskey in my car

Now the name of the hotel seems strange
from the other side of the border
and I'm almost smug as I notice
a mountie giving a speeding ticket
to a car from Colorado
                              I know
they'll be unhappy about the fine
but thrilled by his legendary courtesy

In northern Wyoming
the highway moved through an oil field
still in use as grazing land:
cattle and horses browsed around
derricks and pumps.
I braked the car when a mare and colt
wandered onto the road.
They stared at me, and I thought,
here is the past, looking at the present.
Then I remembered that grass will come up
when the wells are sputtering straws
in an empty bottle. Here was the present,
stopped by the future.
Perhaps my car should have bolted
and wrecked itself in a ditch,
but when the horses skittered
back to their field, I brought
the speedometer smoothly up to 55,
all the parts of the engine humming,
moving freely in a bath of hot oil.

FOG, BRIDGE, FLUTE SONATA

Nothing but fog ahead of the car
In the back seat my two daughters
On the radio a flute sonata

I remember my old notions as a child
riding in the fog or the dark
The feeling that the road will never end

As we reach the long bridge
I try out an idea on my daughters
They're old enough not to believe me

I ask if the river has a far bank
We see nothing but fog yielding to fog
and may ride the bridge forever

Margaret tells me not to be silly
"There has to be another side
or what's holding up the bridge?"

Ah, how can she be skeptical
when she plays the flute herself
and hardly touches the mouthpiece

BACK SEAT PILOT

I have an axiom about the equality of times

As the Champ took off from the grassy strip
Joe waggled its wings to Harriet
down in the car doing her math homework

The highways were a fine set of geometrical shapes
I noticed an interchange like an infinity sign
with the ray of a freeway bisecting its middle

and could have believed our vector was unlimited
except when an occasional bump of warm air
from a plowed field reminded me of earthly ties

After the landing we went back to the car
and tapped on the glass to get Harriet's attention
She had spent a dull half hour on one assignment

Times equal to the same time are not equal to each other

BREAKING LOOSE

1

Glass globes, floats lost from nets
carried by the Kuroshio current from Japan
clear glass, beached like monstrous eggs
or parts from a Martian spacecraft
safe all those miles, a few scratches
from the rough approach to the shore

Size of a fist, size of a skull
trademarked with crisscross characters
the dumb message of another world
no one sends them back
                              boys smash them
collectors fashion nets, or hang them
clustered like grapes from the ceiling

2

I float in stagnant waters, becalmed
a cork bobber with a barbed tongue
I always surface, a string draws me in

Suppose I turned glass, got lost in open water
feeling out currents, passing blind fish
and glowing monsters, finding rocks at last
to shatter on in sight of shore, or easy beach
to wash up, brittle-naked on the sand
a sea-trove for whose strange hands
whose eyes to read the scratches on my skin

IV. POET ON EXPENSE ACCOUNT

Waiting for the airport bus
in the MacDonald Hotel,
I notice the bellhop
lining up white letters
on the announcement board.
The Christians (Reformed)
are meeting in one room,
the Lions in another.
The Rotorians (Misspelled)
hold the line between them.

Riding the bus in the dark
I see the red luminous sign
over the driver's head:
Watch Your Step.
I always will. We pass
the red grain elevator
painted with JESUS SAID,
What Shall It Profit A Man
If He Gain The Whole World
And Lose His Own Soul?
Floodlights keep the message
shining in the darkness,
and I agree, without believing
in Jesus or the soul.

When the sign in the cabin
says Fasten Seat Belts,
I do. And think how careful
the bellhop should be,
with every word in the language
resting in his tray of letters.

The day we hit human reproduction
the classroom was full and sweating
The teacher was known for irreverent wit
He began by speaking of the menstrual cycle
as "the tears of a heart-broken uterus"
The woman in front of me dropped her pencil
but sat very still
              "You fellows there
in the third row: the girl between you
has fainted — help her outside please"
After they did he went on briskly
to his next simile which had the egg
waiting by the lamp post for a sailor

I gave up biology the next year
Sawing through the skull of a cat
persuaded me it was silly to call
the analysis of poems "dissection"
In fourteen years of teaching English
I have never made any student faint
over a line of bad poetry

The poet has been told to charge his meal
to the Public Library
He feels important, almost a businessman
although the restaurant is so fancy
he doesn't know how to act
The shapely glass he holds up for the ice water
turns out to be a tall chimney for the candle
The food comes in substantial portions
a basin of soup, a platter of salad
There's a loaf of bread for a peasant family
and he saws off a slab with the special knife
The relishes arrive in a boat-shaped dish
manned by celery and carrot sticks
stuffed and unstuffed olives, six pickles
and three big peppers, one of them red
He has an obligation to this food
The scallops are served in ceramic sea shells
and come with both rice and potatoes
He could starch his shirts (and the bread
still crouches in the basket under a napkin)
But if he were a genuine businessman
it would be just another merger
a takeover by a multinational corp. —
Ah, there goes bread, there go pickles
and he hardly noticed the potatoes
Look at this delightful napkin
the shade of milk chocolate   oops
and the matching tablecloth slithers down
followed by the pot of ferns near his chair
Now the manager is on the phone to security
The poet hears him yell "Code Red!"
but the table leg is so tasty
No, the poet comes to his senses
waves away the pastries and flaming drinks
even the scooped melon heaped with strawberries
A heel of bread remains in the basket
and five pickles are lying seasick
in the bottom of the glass boat

the writers' convention delegates
line up in the lobby for name tags
with the legend HELLO — MY NAME IS ...
We're ready for serious talking all day
and a little serious drinking at night
I look out the lobby window and see
a white sloop come sailing by
with the name REALITY on its stern
We're looking for it in here — come back!
The pilot has one hand on the wheel
and the other holds a bottle of beer
as the boat moves off into the harbor
On such a sunny day I couldn't blame
reality for wanting to escape from us

MADAM CHAIRMAN, HONORED GUESTS

We're here to honor gifted children
by launching a volume of their writings
With folded arms three politicians sit
on folding chairs in the little theatre
Each one represents someone important
who couldn't come but wanted to be here

An interpreter transforms every speech
into the fluent gestures of the deaf
The politicians have good words for the book
but their speeches are made of pre-fab phrases
many of them damaged in the assembly
"This is a warm-heartening event"
we're told
           and the interpreter
makes a quick move with the hand
fingers outward away from the mouth
then traces the outline of a heart
with index fingers on the chest
I'm astounded to see a speech
gaining so much in the translation

LOOK THIS WAY PLEASE

A red light means the camera is on

The only trouble with the medium
is that it makes everything medium
Coming to honor poetry I am given
ten minutes between the ten minutes each
for Home Security and Fitness Fun

The police can show six basic locks
each mounted in a section of door
They caution against paranoia
but point out all the dangers
While I'm digging in the garden
someone could be in the living room
My paranoia goes them one farther
If I'm in the living room
someone could be in the garden
pulling up unsecured radishes

In my ten minutes I show books
that open freely on their hinges
I'm treated with great courtesy
but don't stay for Fitness Fun
I pick my way out over the cables
Poetry is not breaking and entering
It is a message slipped under the door
You don't even have to read it
It wants to tell you about danger
life and death and good parties
A message slipped under your door